basic Thaï cooking

Jody Vassallo

photography Deirdre Rooney

basic Thaï cooking

whitecap

c o n t e n t s

introduction

Thai food has increased in popularity over the past ten years. I'm not sure whether this is because so many people have travelled to the amazing country and fallen in love with the cuisine as I did, or because they have a favorite restaurant in their neighborhood and have become hooked on fish cakes, pad thai or masaman curry. What I do know is that it is an easy cuisine to learn to cook, and most of it is quick and easy. Probably the thing that takes the longest time is shopping – but that is actually a joy in itself, sifting through Asian supermarkets. Try to get lovely, fresh ingredients as they make a huge difference. You don't need a lot of expensive equipment either, just a wok, mortar and pestle, steamer and a good sharp knife.

Read the glossary thoroughly before you begin, as all the information you need to know about ingredients and how to prepare them is in there. Most importantly, get to know your chilies – the biggest mistake people make is ending up with their dishes too spicy. Remember, you can always add more spice or do as the Thais do and serve sliced fresh chilies to the side for those who like it hotter. If you enjoy curries then I can only encourage you to make your own pastes – it is a labor of love but is thoroughly worthwhile as the flavor of shop-bought paste simply can't compare. However, if you are short on time the commercial pastes will suffice, just make sure you check the heat of the paste as I often find the packaged ones have much more heat than homemade versions – especially green.

Thais are about the only people in Asia who use a spoon and fork to eat their meals. Traditionally food is pushed onto the spoon with the fork and the fork doesn't ever go into the mouth. Chopsticks are used to eat noodle dishes such as pad thai, pad siewe and noodle soups.

So, why not pop on an apron, invite a few friends round and use this book to cook up a storm. I am sure every dish you make will be *Aroi muk muk* ("delicious"), and your guests will be asking to take any leftovers home.

thai ingredients

glutinous rice

spring roll wrappers

dried rice stick noodles

dried glass noodles

black glutinous rice

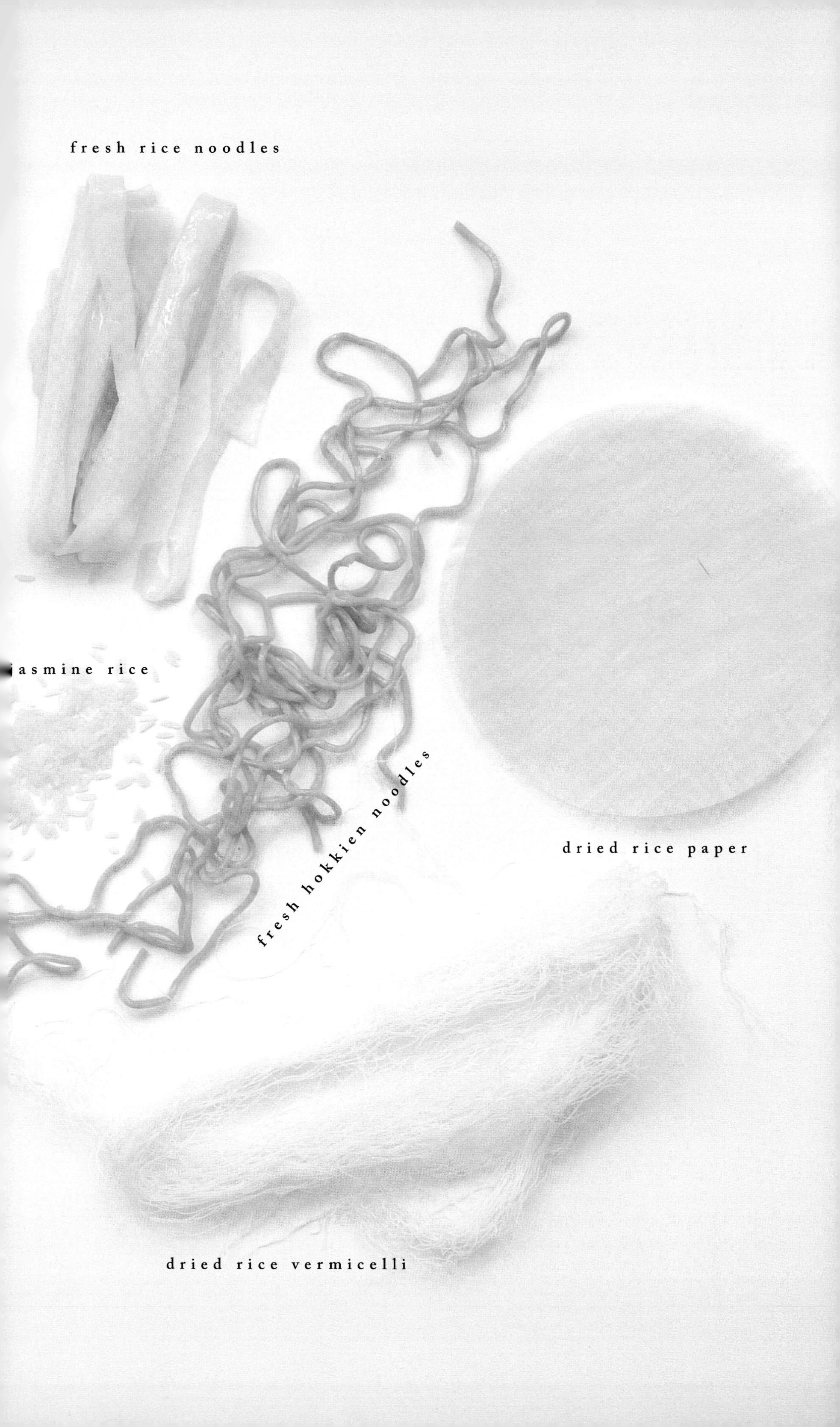

fresh rice noodles

jasmine rice

fresh hokkien noodles

dried rice paper

dried rice vermicelli

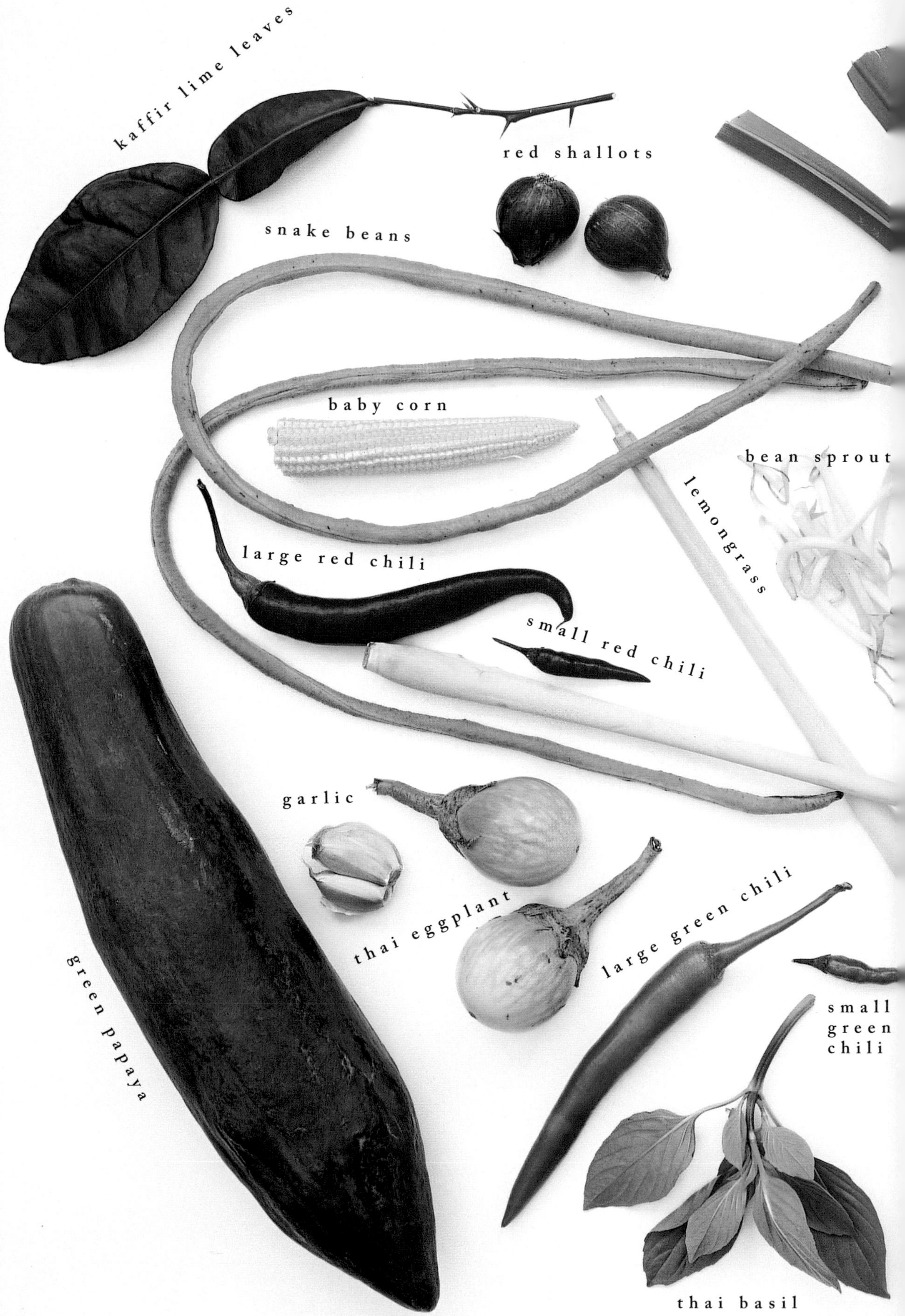

kaffir lime leaves

red shallots

snake beans

baby corn

bean sprout

large red chili

lemongrass

small red chili

garlic

green papaya

thai eggplant

large green chili

small
green
chili

thai basil

thai ingredients

galangal

oyster
mushroom

turmeric

pea eggplant

cilantro

green
peppercorns

kaffir limes

pandanus leaf

ginger

chinese cabbage

tofu

dried red chili

sweet chili sauce

tamarind pulp

shrimp paste

light soy sauce

dried shrimp

palm sugar

thai ingredients

deep-fried garlic

ster sauce

coconut cream

hite peppercorns

coconut milk

fish sauce

bamboo shoots

curry powder

wire sieve

grater

juicer

steamer

short spatula

wok charn

peeler

cleaver

wok brush

mortar and pestle

14

Stock your shelves with: jasmine rice, white and black sticky rice, oyster sauce, fish sauce, noodles, sweet chili sauc

coconut milk, dried shrimp, shrimp paste, soy sauce, chili jam, tamarind, palm sugar, bamboo shoots, dried chili.

how to season a wok

A wok is one of the most essential pieces of kitchen equipment you need for Asian cooking. The best thing about woks is that they are cheap. There is no need to spend a fortune on a fancy wok, a simple carbon steel wok will do the job perfectly. I prefer a wok with a long wooden handle as I find the metal handles get too hot.

After buying a wok you need to season it before use, in order to stop food sticking to it and to prevent it from rusting. When you first get your carbon steel wok home you will need to remove the machine oil they apply at the factory. To do this, wash the wok in soapy water. (If you have a wok that you purchased a while ago and have never seasoned it then it is a good idea to do it now.) Scrub away the rust then proceed:

Once you have washed the wok in soapy water, rinse it under cold water and dry it well.

Brush the entire surface inside of the wok with peanut oil and place it over a high flame. Tilt the wok to heat the sides and burn the oil onto them. Turn off the heat and allow the wok to cool.

Once the wok has cooled mop up any of the excess oil with some absorbent kitchen paper and then begin the process again, brushing, heating and cooling.

Repeat this process about 3 times, making sure that you always wipe any excess oil that pools in the bottom or it will become a thick gel-like layer. You will know when your wok is ready to use as it starts to darken.

General care

After cooking do not wash a seasoned wok in soapy water, simply use a wok brush and brush the wok clean under hot water. The first few times you use your wok it is a good idea to also season it. Dry it over a high flame and then coat with a layer of oil and cook the oil on as you did when you first seasoned the wok, allow it cool then wipe any excess oil off before storing.

After a few months of use the wok will develop a shiny black surface and then it is no longer necessary to season it after using. Simply wash it under cold water and dry it over a high flame.

WASHING a brand new wok in soapy water

BRUSHING a wok with oil

BURNING oil onto a wok

WIPING out excess oil with absorbent kitchen paper

SEASONED wok

CLEANING with a wok brush

how to cook rice

The easiest way to cook perfect rice every time is to buy yourself a rice cooker – after all, millions of Chinese, Thais and Japanese could not be wrong! If, however, you are a purist and you insist on cooking your rice on the stovetop, here is how it is done. It is much easier to cook rice on a gas stovetop rather than an electric one as the temperature is much easier to control. (This is why, if I am cooking on electric, I usually remove the rice once it forms tunnels and allow it to steam off the heat, which saves risking it sticking on the bottom.)

First you need to decide how much rice and the type of rice you want to cook. Thais favor long-grain fragrant jasmine rice to serve with most meals. This is widely available in supermarkets and will give a much more authentic meal than basmati rice, which is more suitable for Indian cooking.

If you start off with 1 cup (250 mL) of uncooked rice, remember that the cooking water will be absorbed and so you will end up with approximately 3 cups (750 mL) of cooked rice. This means approximately 1½ cups (375 mL) of uncooked rice is enough to serve 4 hungry people with a main meal.

Rinse the rice before you cook it, just to remove any grit. Place the drained, rinsed rice into a pan – make sure that it is large enough to hold the cooked expanded volume of rice, as if the pan is too small the rice will have no room to move and will stick together. Add the water and bring it to a boil, then boil it, uncovered, until you see tunnels appear in the rice (which usually takes 3–5 minutes). Turn the heat down as low as it will go, cover the pan and cook for 10 minutes. Remove the rice from the heat and allow it to stand for 5 minutes before serving.

Tip: Another tried and tested way of measuring how much rice to water you need is to put the rice into a pan, then pour in enough water to come up to your knuckle on your thumb when it is rested on the rice.

FRAGRANT jasmine rice

RINSING rice

WATER covering rice

TUNNELS in rice

COVERED rice

STEAMED rice

curry pastes

One of the most important things to consider when you are making a curry paste is that fresh ingredients produce the best-quality paste. Also buy yourself a good size mortar and pestle (it should hold 2 cups/500 mL). There is nothing more frustrating than trying to pound a paste only to have the contents of the bowl keep spilling out onto the counter. I find the best mortar and pestles are the heavy stone ones you can purchase at Asian stores.

PREPARING PASTES

The best thing to do is set a morning aside to buy the ingredients then the afternoon to prepare them – remembering that curries will always taste better reheated. Take the time to chop the ingredients before adding them to the mortar, not too finely but so they will all fit in. Roast your spices, if the paste calls for this, so they are nice and fragrant. Do this slowly as burnt spices will taint the flavor of your paste (this is also the time to roast peanuts (separately) if the recipe asks for them). Then smash away – making pastes requires a little muscle power and patience! It is recommended that you crush each ingredient one at a time for the best flavor. It will take about 10 minutes pounding and scraping down the sides with a spoon to produce a gorgeous amalgamated paste.

STORING PASTES

If you are going to use the paste right away add the shrimp paste, if not store it in an airtight container and add the paste before cooking. Curry pastes do freeze so you can put leftovers in an airtight container and store them for up to 1 month or you can refrigerate them for 2 weeks.

green curry paste

2 teaspoons cumin seeds
1½ tablespoons coriander seeds
4 star anise
2 teaspoons black peppercorns
1 teaspoon dried turmeric (optional)
1½ tablespoons chopped garlic
1½ tablespoons chopped lemongrass
1½ tablespoons chopped fresh coriander root
2 large green chilies, chopped
2 cups cilantro leaves
1 teaspoon shrimp paste

Put the cumin seeds, coriander seeds, star anise and peppercorns into a frying pan and cook for 3 minutes or until fragrant. Transfer to a mortar and pestle or food processor, add the turmeric, if using, and pound or process to form a fine powder.

Add the remaining ingredients one at a time, making sure that each ingredient is thoroughly incorporated before adding the next.

If you are intending to use the curry paste right away, add the shrimp paste and pound or process to combine. If, however, you intend to store the curry paste and use it later do not add the shrimp paste to the paste, leave it until you are going to cook the paste.

Preparation time: 40 minutes – Cooking time: 3 minutes – Makes ½ cup (125 mL)

red curry paste

7 dried long red chilies
1 teaspoon sea salt
1½ tablespoons chopped fresh or dried galangal
3 tablespoons chopped lemongrass
1 teaspoon finely grated kaffir lime rind
5½ tablespoons chopped red shallots
1½ tablespoons chopped fresh coriander root
3 tablespoons chopped garlic
½ teaspoon shrimp paste (optional)

Split the dried red chilies down the center and remove the seeds and white membranes (this is best done while wearing plastic gloves). Soak the chilies in cold water for 15 minutes. Drain and pat dry on absorbent kitchen paper. Put the chilies and the salt into a food processor or mortar and pestle and pound or process until finely ground. Add the remaining ingredients one at a time, making sure that each ingredient is thoroughly incorporated before adding the next. If you are intending to use the curry paste straight away, add the shrimp paste and pound or process to combine. If, however, you intend to store the curry paste and use it later do not add the shrimp paste to the paste, leave it until you are going to cook the paste.

Preparation time: 15 minutes, plus 15 minutes soaking – Cooking time: none – Makes ½ cup (125 mL)

masaman curry paste

6 large dried red chilies
3 white cardamom pods or ½ teaspoon cardamom powder
1 teaspoon cumin seeds
1 tablespoon coriander seeds
5 cloves
¾ inch (2 cm) piece cassia bark or cinnamon
½ teaspoon grated nutmeg
1 teaspoon sea salt
1½ tablespoons chopped fresh or dried galangal
3 tablespoons chopped lemongrass
1 tablespoon chopped fresh coriander root
¼ cup chopped Asian shallots
5½ tablespoons chopped garlic
3 tablespoons chopped roasted peanuts

Split the dried red chilies down the center and remove the seeds and white membranes (this is best done while wearing plastic gloves). Soak the chilies in cold water for 15 minutes. Drain and pat dry on absorbent kitchen paper. Put the cardamom, cumin, coriander seeds, cloves and cassia bark or cinnamon into a frying pan and roast until fragrant, which takes around 2 minutes. Transfer to a mortar and pestle or food processor, add the nutmeg and pound or process to combine. Add the remaining ingredients one at a time, including the soaked chilies, making sure each ingredient is thoroughly incorporated before adding the next.

Preparation time: 20 minutes, plus 15 minutes soaking – Cooking time: 5 minutes – Makes ½ cup (125 mL)

Penang curry paste

8 large dried red chilies
1 teaspoon cumin seeds
1 teaspoon coriander seeds
½ teaspoon black peppercorns
1½ tablespoons chopped lemongrass
2 teaspoons chopped fresh or dried galangal
1 teaspoon chopped fresh coriander root
1½ tablespoons chopped garlic

1½ tablespoons chopped red shallots
1½ tablespoons chopped roasted peanuts
½ teaspoon shrimp paste

Split the dried red chilies down the center and remove the seeds and white membranes (this is best done while wearing plastic gloves). Soak the chilies in cold water for 15 minutes. Drain and pat dry on absorbent kitchen paper. Put the cumin, coriander and peppercorns into a frying pan and cook over a medium heat until fragrant, which takes around 2 minutes. Transfer to a mortar and pestle or food processor and process or pound to a fine powder. Add the remaining ingredients one at a time, including the soaked chilies, making sure each ingredient is thoroughly incorporated before adding the next.

Preparation time: 20 minutes, plus 15 minutes soaking – Cooking time: 5 minutes – Makes ½ cup (125 mL)

yellow curry paste

3 large dried red chilies
1 teaspoon cumin seeds
2 teaspoons coriander seeds
2 teaspoons peeled chopped fresh turmeric or 1 teaspoon yellow curry powder
1½ tablespoons chopped red shallots or red onion
1½ tablespoons chopped garlic
1½ tablespoons chopped lemongrass
2 teaspoons chopped fresh or dried galangal
½ teaspoon salt
½ teaspoon shrimp paste

Split the dried red chilies down the center and remove the seeds and white membranes (this is best done while wearing plastic gloves). Soak the chilies in cold water for 15 minutes. Drain and pat them dry on absorbent kitchen paper. Put the cumin and coriander into a frying pan and cook over a medium heat until fragrant, which takes around 2 minutes. Transfer to a mortar and pestle or food processor, add the turmeric or curry powder and pound or process to a fine powder. Add the remaining ingredients one at a time, including the soaked chilies, making sure each ingredient is thoroughly incorporated before adding the next.

Preparation time: 20 minutes, plus 15 minutes soaking – Cooking time: 5 minutes – Makes ½ cup (125 mL)

chili jam – nam prik pao

2 cups vegetable oil
1 cup peeled garlic
1 cup peeled red shallots or red onion
10 large dried chilies, seeded and chopped
½ cup dried shrimp
½ teaspoon shrimp paste
½ cup grated palm sugar or brown sugar
3 tablespoons tamarind water

Pour the oil into a wok and heat until it starts to move. Test it by standing a wooden chopstick upright in the oil – if it bubbles around the chopstick it is ready to use. Cook the garlic until golden, then drain on absorbent kitchen paper. Cook the shallotsor onion until golden, then drain on absorbent kitchen paper. Cook the chilies until crisp, drain then cook the shrimp until golden and drain as before.Wrap the shrimp paste in foil and cook in a clean frying pan until fragrant, which takes 1–2 minutes. Put the deep-fried ingredients and shrimp paste into a food processor with approximately 1⁄2 cup of the cooled cooking oil and blend to form a paste.Put the paste into a pan, add the sugar and tamarind water and cook, stirring a few times, over a medium heat until thick and sticky. Do not overcook or it will become too firm on standing.

Preparation time: 20 minutes – Cooking time: 30 minutes – Makes 1½ cups (375 mL)

LEFT TO RIGHT: PENANG CURRY PASTE, CHILI JAM
(NAM PRIK PAO), YELLOW CURRY PASTE

LEFT TO RIGHT: GREEN CURRY PASTE, RED CURRY PASTE,
MASAMAN CURRY PASTE

soups and starters

deep-fried spring rolls

1⅔ oz (50 g) dried glass noodles or Chinese vermicelli
1½ tablespoons (22 mL) peanut oil
3½ oz (100 g) raw prawn meat, chopped
1½ tablespoons (22 mL) fresh ginger, grated
1 clove garlic, crushed
½ cup (125 mL) Chinese cabbage, finely sliced
2 cups (500 mL) carrot, grated
¼ cup (60 mL) fresh cilantro leaves
1½ tablespoons (22 mL) spring onions, finely sliced
1½ tablespoons (22 mL) fish sauce
1½ tablespoons (22 mL) oyster sauce
12 spring roll wrappers
1 teaspoon (5 mL) cornstarch mixed with 2 tablespoons (30mL) water
2 cups (500 mL) peanut oil, for frying
sweet chili sauce, for dipping

Put the noodles into a bowl, cover with hot water and allow to stand for 5 minutes or until soft. Drain well. Use scissors to cut the noodles into short lengths. Heat the oil in a wok, add the prawn, ginger and garlic and stir-fry until golden. Add the cabbage, carrot, cilantro leaves, spring onions, glass noodles or vermicelli, fish sauce and oyster sauce. Cook for 3 minutes then allow to cool for about 20 minutes.

Lay a spring roll wrapper out onto a flat surface, place 2 tablespoons of the mixture onto one end and roll it up, enclosing the sides as you go. Brush the edge with the cornstarch mix and press to seal. Repeat the process for the remaining spring roll wrappers.

Pour the oil into a wok and heat until the oil starts to move. You can test if it is ready by standing a wooden chopstick upright in the oil – if it bubbles around the chopstick it is ready. Cook the spring rolls in batches (adding too many to the pan at once will lower the oil temperature and the spring rolls will become oily) until crisp and golden, drain on absorbent kitchen paper and keep warm in a moderate oven while you cook the remaining rolls. Serve with the sweet chili sauce.

Preparation time: 45 minutes – Cooking time: 25 minutes, plus 20 minutes cooling –
Makes 12 spring rolls

Spring rolls can be rolled and refrigerated, cook just before serving so they are crisp.

DEEP-FRIED SPRING ROLLS

fish cakes

FOR THE DIPPING SAUCE
1 Lebanese cucumber, seeded and finely diced
1 small red chili, seeded and finely chopped
¼ cup (60 mL) grated palm sugar or brown sugar
⅓ cup + 1 tablespoon (100 mL) rice vinegar
1 tablespoon (15 mL) chopped fresh cilantro

14 oz (400 g) skinless red fish or snapper fillets, chopped
7 oz (200 g) raw prawns, peeled and deveined, chopped
1½–3 tablespoons (22–45 mL) red curry paste (see page 24)
½ cup (125 mL) finely sliced snake beans or green beans
4 kaffir lime leaves, stems removed and finely shredded
2 cups (500 mL) peanut oil

To make the dipping sauce, put the cucumber, chili, sugar, 1 tablespoon (15 mL) of water, vinegar and cilantro into a bowl and mix to combine. Set aside while you prepare the fish cakes.

Put the fish and prawns into a mortar and pestle or food processor and pound or process until smooth. Add the curry paste and process until the mixture forms a sticky ball in the food processor or it becomes a really sticky mass in the mortar.

Transfer the mixture to a bowl and fold in the beans and lime leaves. Shape into 18 flat patties or small roughly shaped balls and place onto a baking tray, cover with plastic wrap and chill for 1 hour.

Heat the oil in a wok until it starts to move. You can test it by standing a wooden chopstick upright in the oil – if it bubbles around the chopstick it is ready.

Cook the fish cakes in batches (adding too many to the wok at once will lower the oil temperature and the fish cakes will become oily) until crisp and golden brown. Drain each batch on absorbent kitchen paper and keep warm in a moderate oven while you cook the remaining fish cakes. Serve with the dipping sauce or sweet chili sauce.

Preparation time: 20 minutes, plus 1 hour chilling – Cooking time: 15 minutes – Makes 18

pork and prawn noodle soup

1¾ oz (50 g) dried glass noodles
1 teaspoon (5 mL) chopped fresh coriander root
½ teaspoon (2 mL) white peppercorns
2 teaspoons (10 mL) chopped garlic
1½ tablespoons (22 mL) vegetable oil
3½ oz (100 g) ground pork
8 oz (250 g) raw prawns, peeled and deveined
4 cups (1 L) chicken stock
1½ tablespoons (22 mL) fish sauce
1¾ oz (50 g) oyster mushrooms, sliced
1 spring onion, sliced
1½ tablespoons (22 mL) fresh cilantro leaves
1½ tablespoons (22 mL) deep-fried garlic

Put the noodles into a bowl, cover with cold water and allow to stand for 15 minutes or until soft. Drain well.

Put the coriander root, peppercorns and garlic into a mortar and pestle and pound to form a smooth paste.

Heat the oil in a large pan, add the paste and pork and cook for 5 minutes until the pork is cooked. Add the prawns and cook until pink, which should take about 3 minutes. Add the stock, fish sauce, mushrooms and noodles and simmer for 10 minutes. Finally, stir in the spring onion, cilantro leaves and garlic.

Preparation time: 20 minutes, plus 15 minutes soaking – Cooking time: 20 minutes – Serves 4

pork satay

12 bamboo skewers
1 lb (500 g) pork fillets

FOR THE SATAY SAUCE
2 cups (500 mL) coconut milk
1½ tablespoons (22 mL) red curry paste (see page 24)
1½ tablespoons (22 mL) fish sauce
1½ tablespoons (22 mL) grated palm sugar or brown sugar
4 oz (125 g) roasted peanuts, ground

Soak the bamboo skewers in cold water for 30 minutes to avoid them burning when they are placed on the barbecue grill.

Pound the pork until it is ¾ inch (2 cm) thick and cut it into thick strips. Weave the pork strips onto the bamboo skewers.

To make the satay sauce, put the coconut milk and curry paste into a pan and cook, stirring constantly, until the coconut milk comes to the boil. Add the fish sauce, sugar and peanuts and cook, stirring constantly, until the sauce boils and thickens.

Cook the skewers on a lightly oiled barbecue grill or griddle pan until tender. Serve with the satay sauce.

Preparation time: 20 minutes, plus 30 minutes soaking – Cooking time: 30 minutes – Serves 4

Pounding the pork will help it cook faster – and remember to soak the skewers.

PORK SATAY

vegetable curry puffs

2 cloves garlic
1½ tablespoons (22 mL) chopped fresh ginger
1½ tablespoons (22 mL) chopped fresh coriander root
1 teaspoon (5 mL) sea salt
½ teaspoon (2 mL) white pepper
3 tablespoons (45 mL) curry powder
1½ tablespoons (22 mL) grated palm sugar or brown sugar
3 tablespoons (45 mL) vegetable oil
3 potatoes (around 14 oz/400 g), peeled and finely diced
4 sweet potatoes (around 10 oz/300 g), peeled and finely diced
½ cup (125 mL) peas, fresh or frozen
3 tablespoons (45 mL) spring onions, finely sliced
3 tablespoons (45 mL) fresh cilantro leaves, chopped
3 puff pastry sheets, slightly thawed
1¾ cups (400 mL) vegetable oil
sweet chili sauce, to serve

Put the garlic, ginger, coriander root, salt, white pepper, curry powder and sugar into a mortar and pestle and pound to form a paste. Heat the oil in a non-stick frying pan over a medium heat, add the paste and cook until fragrant, which takes about 3 minutes. Add the potatoes, sweet potato and peas and cook for 10 minutes with the lid on. Add the spring onions and cilantro, mix them in well and remove the pan from the heat. Leave to cool for about 20 minutes.

Cut 5 inch (12 cm) circles from the pastry using a fluted cutter. Lay one circle flat and place 1 tablespoon (15 mL) of the filling in the middle of the circle. Brush the edges with water and fold over to enclose the filling. Seal the edges with your fingers, pinching the pastry to form a curly border. Put a twist in each corner of the pastry. Set aside on parchment paper, and repeat until all the mixture is finished.

Pour the oil into a wok or saucepan and heat until the oil starts to move. You can test if it is ready by standing a wooden chopstick upright in the oil – if it bubbles around the chopstick it is ready. Deep-fry the vegetable puffs in batches (adding too many to the pan at once will lower the oil temperature and the puffs will become oily) until crisp and golden brown. Drain on absorbent kitchen paper and serve with sweet chili sauce.

Preparation time: 45 minutes – Cooking time: 30 minutes, plus 20 minutes cooling – Makes 24

pork and peanut dip

1 teaspoon (5 mL) fresh coriander root
2 shallots, chopped
1 small red chili, seeded
2 cloves garlic, chopped
¼ cup (60 mL) roasted, unsalted peanuts, chopped
3 tablespoons (45 mL) peanut oil
5 oz (150 g) ground pork
½ cup (125 mL) coconut milk
3 tablespoons (45 mL) crunchy peanut butter
1½ tablespoons (22 mL) fish sauce
1½ tablespoons (22 mL) grated palm sugar or brown sugar
fresh cilantro leaves, to garnish

In a mortar and pestle pound the coriander root, shallots, chili, garlic and peanuts. Heat the oil in a wok or frying pan, add the mixture and fry until fragrant (which takes about 2 minutes). Add the pork and cook for 2–3 minutes or until the pork is cooked.

Pour in the coconut milk, peanut butter, fish sauce and sugar and bring to the boil. Reduce the heat and simmer for 10 minutes.

Serve the dip in a bowl, garnished with the cilantro. Try accompanying the dip with fried toast or vegetable strips.

Preparation time: 10 minutes – Cooking time: 20 minutes – Serves 4

rice paper rolls

3½ oz (100 g) rice vermicelli
20 rice paper rounds 6½ inches (16 cm) in diameter
20 cooked king prawns, peeled and deveined then halved
2 cups (500 mL) shredded lettuce
1 carrot, finely shredded
40 fresh mint leaves
sweet chili sauce, to serve

Put the vermicelli into a bowl, cover with hot water and allow to stand for 10 minutes or until soft. Drain well and cut into short lengths.

Soak a rice paper round in warm water until soft. Place onto a clean tea towel.

Place a heaped tablespoon of the noodles along one edge of the rice paper round, top with 2 prawn halves, some lettuce and carrot and 2 mint leaves. Fold in the sides and roll up to enclose. Cover with absorbent kitchen paper to prevent it drying out while you prepare the remaining rolls.

Serve with sweet chili sauce.

Preparation time: 30 minutes, plus 10 minutes standing – Cooking time: none – Makes 20

Keep the rolls covered with absorbent kitchen paper to keep them moist.

RICE PAPER ROLLS

tom kai gai

3 cups (750 mL) coconut milk
1½ tablespoons (22 mL) finely sliced galangal (approximately 5 slices)
1 lemongrass stalk, bruised and finely sliced
1½ tablespoons (22 mL) finely chopped red shallots or red onion
4 small red chilies, halved
10 oz (300 g) chicken breast, thinly sliced
3½ oz (100 g) fresh oyster mushrooms, halved
2 whole kaffir lime leaves, stems removed and leaves torn
1½–3 tablespoons (22–45 mL) fish sauce
1½ tablespoons (22 mL) lime juice
fresh cilantro leaves, to garnish

Put the coconut milk into a pan and bring to the boil, stirring constantly, in order to stop the coconut milk from cracking (separating out).

Once the coconut milk has boiled, add the galangal, lemongrass, shallots or onion and chilies, bring to a boil and cook for 5 minutes. Reduce the heat to a simmer.

Add the chicken, mushrooms, lime leaves and fish sauce and cook for 5 minutes or until the chicken is tender. Turn off the heat, add the lime juice and cilantro and stir to combine.

Preparation time: 15 minutes – Cooking time: 15 minutes – Serves 4

prawn balls

2 teaspoons (10 mL) chopped garlic
1 teaspoon (5 mL) chopped fresh coriander root
½ teaspoon (2 mL) white peppercorns
½ teaspoon (2 mL) superfine sugar
1 lb (500 g) raw prawns, peeled and deveined
1½ tablespoons (22 mL) chopped fresh cilantro leaves
2 cups (500 mL) peanut oil, for deep-frying

Put the garlic, coriander root, peppercorns and sugar into a mortar and pestle or food processor and pound or process to a smooth paste. Add the prawns and pound or process until smooth. Stir in the cilantro leaves and mix to combine.

Shape tablespoons of the mixture into balls and place onto a baking tray lined with parchment paper, cover with plastic wrap and chill for 30 minutes.

Pour the oil into a wok and heat until the oil starts to move. You can test if it is ready by standing a wooden chopstick upright in the oil – if it bubbles around the chopstick it is ready.

Cook the prawn balls in batches (adding too many to the pan at once will lower the oil temperature and the balls will become oily) until crisp and golden brown. Drain each batch on absorbent kitchen paper and keep warm in a moderate oven while you cook the remaining prawn balls. Serve hot.

Preparation time: 30 minutes, plus 30 minutes chilling – Cooking time: 10 minutes – Makes 12

tom yum goong

1 lb (500 g) raw prawns
1½ tablespoons (22 mL) vegetable oil
2 stalks lemongrass, bruised and finely sliced
3 slices galangal (optional)
1½ tablespoons (22 mL) finely chopped red shallot or red onion
3 small red chilies, halved
1½–3 tablespoons (22–45 mL) chili jam (nam prik pao – see page 25)
2 whole kaffir lime leaves, stems discarded and torn
8 cherry tomatoes, halved
3½ oz (100 g) button mushrooms, halved
3 tablespoons (45 mL) fish sauce
2 tablespoons (30 mL) lime juice

Peel and devein the prawns, leaving the tails. Don't throw away the shells as you will use them to make the stock for the soup.

Heat the oil in a deep saucepan or wok, add the prawn shells and cook them until they turn pink, which takes around 3–5 minutes. Add 5 cups (1.25 L) of water and bring to a boil. Cook for 5 minutes then strain, saving the liquid and discarding the shells.

Return the stock to the pan, add the lemongrass, galangal (if using), shallot or onion, chilies, chili jam and kaffir lime leaves and bring to a boil. Boil for 5 minutes before reducing the heat to a simmer.

Add the tomatoes and mushrooms and simmer for 5 minutes. Add the prawns and cook until they turn pink, which takes 3–5 minutes. Turn off the heat and stir in the fish sauce and lime juice.

Preparation time: 25 minutes – Cooking time: 25 minutes – Serves 4

vegetables

mee grob

2 cups (500 mL) peanut oil, for deep-frying
5 oz (150 g) dried glass noodles or Chinese vermicelli, cut into small pieces
2 eggs, lightly beaten
3 cloves garlic, chopped
8 oz (250 g) tofu, diced
3 spring onions, sliced
¼ cup (60 mL) grated palm sugar or brown sugar
3 tablespoons (45 mL) fish sauce or soy sauce for vegetarians
¼ cup (60 mL) lime juice
3 tablespoons (45 mL) white vinegar
1½ tablespoons (22 mL) chopped fresh cilantro
1¾ oz (50 g) bean sprouts, to serve
1 large red chili, finely sliced, to garnish

Pour the oil into a wok and heat until the oil starts to move. You can test if it is ready
by standing a wooden chopstick upright in the oil – if it bubbles around the chopstick
it is ready.

Cook the glass noodles or Chinese vermicelli in small batches (adding too many to
the pan at once will lower the oil temperature and the noodles will become oily) until
puffed crisp and white. Drain on absorbent kitchen paper. Turn off the oil and set it
aside to cool for 30 minutes.

Carefully remove all but 3 tablespoons (45 mL) of the oil from the wok and also reserve
3 extra tablespoons (45 mL) for later – this is best done with a metal ladle. Heat the
oil in the wok, add the egg and swirl so it coats the sides of the wok. Allow the egg to
set then flip it over to cook the other side. Remove the omelette, allow it to cool slightly
and finely shred it into thin strips.

Add the reserved 3 tablespoons (45 mL) of oil, the garlic and tofu to the wok and
stir-fry over a high heat until golden. Add the spring onions and cook until soft.

Add the sugar, fish sauce or soy sauce, lime juice and vinegar and bring to a boil.
Add the noodles and cilantro and quickly toss to coat the noodles in the sauce.

Serve the mee grob topped with the bean sprouts and the shredded egg. Garnish with
sliced red chili.

Preparation time: 30 minutes, plus 30 minutes cooling – Cooking time: 20 minutes – Serves 4

Cook small batches of the noodles in the oil, so they have room to puff up.

MEE GROB

vegetables

vegetable fried rice

3 tablespoons (45 mL) vegetable oil
3 Asian shallots, chopped
4 cloves garlic, chopped
1½ tablespoons (22 mL) grated palm sugar or brown sugar
3½ oz (100 g) green beans, sliced
3½ oz (100 g) fresh or frozen peas
½ red bell pepper, finely sliced
1 ripe tomato, chopped
4 spring onions, sliced
3 eggs, lightly beaten
3½ oz (100 g) bean sprouts
4 cups (1 L) cooled cooked jasmine rice
1½ tablespoons (22 mL) light soy sauce
1½ tablespoons (22 mL) dark soy sauce
½ cup (125 mL) fresh cilantro leaves

Heat the oil in a wok over a medium heat and stir-fry the shallots and garlic until the garlic is golden. Add the sugar, beans, peas, red bell pepper, tomato and spring onions and stir-fry for 3 minutes. Push to one side, add the beaten egg and cook until slightly scrambled. Add the bean sprouts, rice, soy sauces and cilantro leaves and stir-fry on a high heat until heated through. Serve immediately.

Preparation time: 20 minutes – Cooking time: 15 minutes – Serves 4

som tam - green papaya salad with peanuts and chili

2 cloves garlic
1 long red chili, seeded and chopped
1 oz (30 g) unsalted roasted peanuts
1½ tablespoons (22 mL) dried shrimp
2 tablespoons (30 mL) grated palm sugar or brown sugar
¼ cup (60 mL) lime juice
3 tablespoons (45 mL) fish sauce
3½ oz (100 g) cherry tomatoes
4 cups (1 L) green papaya, peeled and grated
2 shallots, finely sliced
½ cup (125 mL) fresh Thai basil leaves
½ cup (125 mL) fresh cilantro leaves

In a large mortar and pestle pound the garlic and chili to a paste, add the peanuts and pound roughly together. Add the shrimp, sugar, lime juice and fish sauce and mix with the pestle. Add the cherry tomatoes and lightly squash the skins of the tomatoes.

Transfer the mixture to a bowl. Add the papaya, shallots, basil and cilantro and toss well together.

Preparation time: 25 minutes – Cooking time: 10 minutes – Serves 4–6

SOM TAM – GREEN PAPAYA SALAD WITH PEANUTS
AND CHILI

You can use a mandoline or grater to shred the green papaya.

green vegetable and tofu curry

3 tablespoons (45 mL) vegetable oil
8 oz (250 g) firm tofu, thickly sliced
3–4 tablespoons (45–60 mL) green curry paste (see page 22)
2 cups (500 mL) coconut milk – do not stir
3 Thai eggplants or 1 small eggplant, cut into wedges
1 carrot, sliced
1 red bell pepper, sliced
1½ tablespoons (22 mL) grated palm sugar or brown sugar
7 oz (200 g) broccoli, cut into florets
3½ oz (100 g) snow peas
1½ tablespoons (22 mL) lime juice
2 kaffir limes, stems removed and finely shredded, to garnish

Heat the oil in a wok, add the tofu and cook until golden. Add the curry paste and the thickest part of the coconut cream from the top of the can to the wok. Cook, stirring constantly, over a medium heat for 3 minutes or until the oil starts to separate from the cream.

Add the remaining coconut milk, eggplant, carrot, red bell pepper and sugar and bring to a boil. Reduce the heat and simmer for 10 minutes.

Add the broccoli and snow peas to the wok and simmer for 5 minutes or until the broccoli is tender. Turn off the heat and stir in the lime juice. Serve sprinkled with the shredded lime leaves.

Preparation time: 25 minutes – Cooking time: 20 minutes – Serves 4

stir-fried tofu with garlic and pepper

1½ tablespoons (22 mL) vegetable oil
1½ lb (750 g) firm tofu, drained and cut into ¾ inch (2 cm) cubes
1 shallot, finely chopped
5 cloves garlic, crushed
1 teaspoon (5 mL) black peppercorns
1 teaspoon (5 mL) white peppercorns
2 teaspoons (10 mL) superfine sugar
3 tablespoons (45 mL) oyster sauce

Heat the oil in a wok over a medium heat, add the tofu and fry until golden. Add the shallot and garlic and toss for 1 minute.

In a mortar and pestle place the black peppercorns, white peppercorns and sugar and pound together before adding them to the tofu. Pour in the oyster sauce and toss until all the tofu has been coated. Serve immediately.

Preparation time: 10 minutes – Cooking time: 5 minutes – Serves 4

STIR-FRIED TOFU WITH GARLIC AND PEPPER

spicy tofu and peanut satay salad

3 tablespoons (45 mL) vegetable oil
1 long red chili, seeded and finely sliced
2 cloves garlic, sliced
1 lb (500 g) firm tofu, drained and cut into ¾ inch (2 cm) cubes
4 spring onions, cut into 2 inch (5 cm) pieces
3½ oz (100 g) bean shoots
½ small Chinese cabbage, thinly sliced
½ cup (125 mL) fresh Thai basil
½ red bell pepper, thinly sliced
½ cup (125 mL) satay sauce (see page 36)
4 kaffir lime leaves, stems removed and finely sliced, to garnish

Heat the oil in a wok over a medium heat, add the chili and garlic and cook until the garlic turns golden. Add the tofu and cook until the tofu has browned. Add the spring onions and toss for another minute. Remove from the heat.

In a large bowl mix together the bean shoots, cabbage, Thai basil and red bell pepper. Divide this mixture among 4 bowls, top with the tofu and satay sauce and garnish with lime leaves.

Preparation time: 15 minutes – Cooking time: 15 minutes – Serves 4–6

stir-fried mixed vegetables

3 tablespoons (45 mL) vegetable oil
2 cloves garlic, chopped
3½ oz (100 g) sugar snap peas, trimmed
10 baby corn, halved lengthwise
3½ oz (100 g) asparagus, cut into 2 inch (5 cm) lengths
3½ oz (100 g) fresh shitake mushrooms
1 bunch choy sum, Chinese greens or Chinese broccoli, chopped into 2 inch (5 cm)
   pieces
2⅔ oz (80g) garlic chives with flowers, chopped into 2 inch (5 cm) pieces
3 tablespoons oyster sauce
1½ tablespoons sweet chili sauce
½ teaspoon sesame oil
white pepper

Heat the oil in a wok over a medium heat, add the garlic and cook until light brown.
Turn the heat up to high and add the peas, baby corn, asparagus, mushrooms, choy sum,
garlic chives, oyster sauce, sweet chili sauce and sesame oil and stir-fry, constantly
tossing, for 2–3 minutes. Sprinkle with white pepper and serve immediately.

Preparation time: 10 minutes – Cooking time: 10 minutes – Serves 4–6

stir-fried eggplant

3 tablespoons (45 mL) vegetable oil
3 tablespoons (45 mL) fresh ginger, finely sliced
2 cloves garlic, sliced
½ teaspoon (2 mL) crushed chili
4 small eggplants, cut into wedges
3 tablespoons (45 mL) soy sauce
3 tablespoons (45 mL) sweet chili sauce
1½ tablespoons (22 mL) fish sauce
1½ tablespoons (22 mL) grated palm sugar or brown sugar

Heat the oil in a wok over a medium heat, add the ginger, garlic and chili and stir-fry
for 1–2 minutes or until golden. Add the eggplant and stir-fry for 5 minutes.

Add the soy sauce, sweet chili sauce, fish sauce and sugar, bring to a boil and cook for
5 minutes or until the eggplants are soft and golden. Serve on a large plate.

Preparation time: 10 minutes – Cooking time: 15 minutes – Serves 4–6

Buy small eggplants so you will not need to salt them to remove the bitterness.

STIR-FRIED EGGPLANT

vegetables

pad siewe

1 lb (500 g) fresh rice noodles, at room temperature
¼ cup (60 mL) vegetable oil
10 oz (300 g) firm tofu, drained and thinly sliced
4 cloves garlic, crushed
1 carrot, thinly sliced
6½ oz (200 g) cauliflower, cut into small florets
8 oz (250 g) Chinese broccoli or pak choi (bok choy), roughly chopped
4 eggs, lightly beaten

FOR THE SAUCE
¼ cup (60 mL) oyster sauce
2 tablespoons (30 mL) soy sauce
1 teaspoon (5 mL) superfine sugar
1 teaspoon (5 mL) white pepper

Cut the rice noodles into thick slices. Heat the oil in a wok, add the tofu and stir-fry over a high heat until crisp and golden. Add the garlic, carrot and cauliflower and 2 tablespoons of water and stir-fry for 5 minutes. Add the Chinese broccoli or pak choi (bok choy) and cook for 2 minutes. Add the noodles to the wok and stir-fry until they are soft.

Combine the sauce ingredients in a bowl. Pour the mixture into the wok and stir-fry until the sauce coats the noodles. Push the noodles to one side of the wok and add in the beaten egg. Stir-fry the egg until it has set, then combine it with the noodles.

Preparation time: 20 minutes – Cooking time: 15 minutes – Serves 4

sweet and sour vegetables

1½ tablespoons (22 mL) vegetable oil
1 onion, thinly sliced
2 cloves garlic, sliced
6 oz (200 g) chopped fresh pineapple
½ cup (125 mL) chicken or vegetable stock
1 Lebanese cucumber or cucumber, peeled, seeded and thickly sliced
½ red bell pepper, chopped
½ green bell pepper, chopped
3½ oz (100 g) baby corn, halved
1 ripe tomato, cut into wedges
1½ tablespoons (22 mL) fish sauce or soy sauce for vegetarians
3 tablespoons (45 mL) sweet chili sauce
1½ tablespoons (22 mL) tamarind water

Heat the oil in a wok, add the onion and garlic and stir-fry over a medium heat until the onion is soft.

Add the pineapple and 1⁄2 cup (125 mL) of the stock and cook for 2 minutes. Add the cucumber, bell peppers, corn and tomato and the remaining stock and cook for 5 minutes.

Stir in the fish or soy sauce, sweet chili sauce and tamarind and bring to a boil.

Preparation time: 20 minutes – Cooking time: 15 minutes – Serves 4

seafood

chu chi scallop and fish curry

2 cups (500 mL) coconut milk – do not stir
3 tablespoons (45 mL) red curry paste (see page 24)
1 teaspoon (5 mL) shrimp paste, roasted (optional)
3 tablespoons (45 mL) fish sauce
1½–3 tablespoons (22–45 mL) grated palm sugar or brown sugar
4 kaffir lime leaves, stems removed and torn
½ teaspoon (2 mL) white pepper
10 oz (300 g) boneless firm white fish fillets (such as snapper, cod or halibut), cubed
3 tablespoons (45 mL) fresh Thai basil leaves
12 scallops with roe removed

Heat a wok and add the coconut cream from the top of the can as well as the curry paste. Cook over a medium heat for 5 minutes or until the coconut cream cracks (separates out) and the oil floats to the surface. Add the remaining coconut milk.

Season the dish with the shrimp paste (if using), fish sauce, sugar and limes leaves and white pepper. Simmer for 20 minutes or until the curry has reduced and thickened. Add the fish, basil and scallops and cook for 5 minutes, or until tender.

Preparation time: 15 minutes – Cooking time: 30 minutes – Serves 4

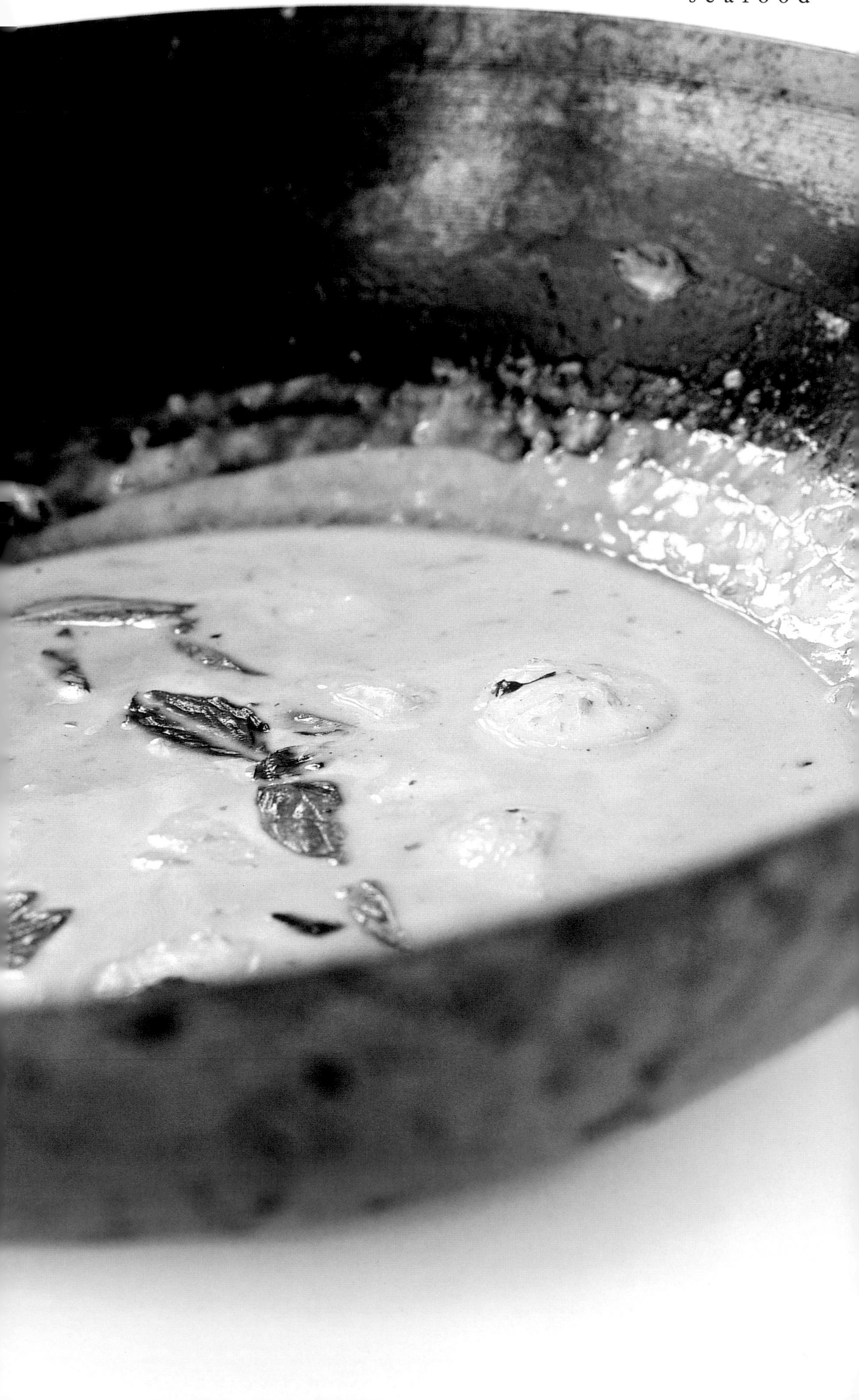

deep-fried fish with sweet sour sauce

FOR THE SAUCE
3 tablespoons (45 mL) soya bean (soybean) oil
¼ cup (60 mL) chopped red shallots or red onion
4 cloves garlic, chopped
3 tablespoons (45 mL) tamarind water
1½ tablespoons (22 mL) fish sauce
½ cup (125 mL) grated palm sugar or brown sugar
¼ cup (60 mL) lime juice

1½ lb (750 g) cleaned whole snapper
4 cups (1 L) peanut oil, for deep-frying

TO GARNISH
1 large red chili, thinly sliced

To make the sauce, heat the soya bean (soybean) oil in a wok, add the shallots or red
onion and garlic and cook over a low heat for 3–5 minutes or until golden.

Add the tamarind water, fish sauce, sugar and lime juice to the wok and simmer for
10 minutes or until the mixture becomes syrupy. Garnish with the sliced chili.

Cut 3 deep incisions on both sides of the fish. Dry on absorbent kitchen paper.

Heat the peanut oil in a wok over a medium heat until the oil starts to move. You can
test if it is ready by standing a wooden chopstick upright in the oil – if it bubbles around
the chopstick it is ready.

Gently lower the fish into the oil and deep-fry for 3–5 minutes each side or until golden
and tender. Remove and drain on absorbent kitchen paper. Serve with the sauce.

Preparation time: 15 minutes – Cooking time: 15 minutes – Serves 4

fried rice with seafood

3 tablespoons (45 mL) vegetable oil
3 tablespoons (45 mL) fresh ginger, chopped
3 cloves garlic, chopped
2 Asian shallots, chopped
10 oz (300 g) raw prawns (shrimp), peeled and deveined
10 oz (300 g) firm white fish (such as snapper, cod or monkfish),
  cut into ¾ inch (2 cm) cubes
10 oz (300 g) calamari, cut into ½ inch x 2 inch (1 cm x 5 cm) strips
1½ tablespoons (22 mL) grated palm sugar or brown sugar
3 tablespoons (45 mL) fish sauce
4 cups (1 L) cooled cooked jasmine rice
1 tomato, chopped
4 spring onions, sliced
3½ oz (100 g) bean sprouts
3 tablespoons (45 mL) fresh cilantro leaves, chopped
3 tablespoons (45 mL) fresh Thai basil leaves, chopped
1 long red chili, seeded and thinly sliced
soy sauce, to serve

Heat the oil in a large wok over a medium heat and stir-fry the ginger, garlic and
shallots for 2 minutes. Add the prawns, fish, calamari, sugar and fish sauce and stir-fry
for 2 minutes.

Add the rice, tomato and spring onions and stir-fry for another 2 minutes. Add the
bean sprouts, cilantro, Thai basil and chili and toss for 1 minute. Serve immediately
with the soy sauce.

Preparation time: 25 minutes – Cooking time: 10 minutes – Serves 4–6

To peel a prawn, remove the head, then the shell from the body.

steamed fish with lemongrass and chili

1 whole cleaned fish (such as red snapper, bass, bream, barramundi,
  pearl perch) – approx 1½ lb (750 g)
1 stalk lemongrass, thinly sliced
1½ tablespoons (22 mL) finely sliced fresh ginger
1 large red chili, seeded and finely chopped
1 large green chili, seeded and finely chopped
3 tablespoons (45 mL) fish sauce
¼ cup (60 mL) lime juice
1½ tablespoons (22 mL) superfine sugar
½ cup (125 mL) chicken stock

TO GARNISH
fresh cilantro leaves
sliced spring onions

Cut 3 deep diagonal incisions into the thickest part of the fish then turn it over and do
the same on the other side.

Place the fish onto a plate and top with the lemongrass and ginger. Put the fish into a
steamer over simmering water, cover and cook for 15 minutes or until the fish flakes
easily when tested with the tip of a knife.

Put the chilies, fish sauce, lime juice, sugar and stock into a bowl and mix until the sugar
dissolves. Pour over the hot fish and garnish with the cilantro and spring onions.

Preparation time: 15 minutes – Cooking time: 15–20 minutes – Serves 4

STEAMED FISH WITH LEMONGRASS AND CHILI

squid with garlic and pepper

1 lb (500 g) cleaned squid tubes
3 tablespoons (45 mL) chopped garlic
1½ tablespoons (22 mL) chopped fresh coriander root
1 teaspoon (5 mL) white peppercorns
½ teaspoon (2 mL) sea salt
2 spring onions, cut into 1¼ inch (3 cm) pieces
3 tablespoons (45 mL) peanut oil
3 tablespoons (45 mL) fish sauce
1½ tablespoons (22 mL) lime juice

Lay the squid tubes out on a flat work surface, with the inside of the tubes facing up.
Angle your knife and make small slices in one direction about 1⁄2 inch (1 cm) apart.
Rotate the board 90 degrees and make small slices in the squid in the opposite direction
– this will produce a honeycomb effect.

Put the garlic, coriander root, peppercorns and salt into a mortar and pestle or spice
grinder and pound or grind to a paste.

Heat the oil in a wok and add the squid. Stir-fry until the squid has curled and is white.
Add the paste and continue to cook until the squid is just cooked through.

Add the spring onions and fish sauce and cook for 2 minutes. Turn off the heat and stir
in the lime juice.

Preparation time: 25 minutes – Cooking time: 10 minutes – Serves 4

sweet chili prawns with basil

1½ tablespoons (22 mL) vegetable oil
2 lb (1 kg) raw prawns, peeled and deveined
2 sprigs fresh green peppercorns
3 cloves garlic, chopped
3 tablespoons (45 mL) chili jam (nam prik pao – see page 25)
  or chili bean paste in soya bean (soybean) oil
4 kaffir lime leaves, stems removed and finely shredded
⅓ cup (80 mL) fish sauce
¼ cup (60 mL) grated palm sugar or brown sugar
¼ cup (60 mL) fresh Thai basil leaves

TO GARNISH
1 large red chili, seeded and thinly sliced
2 tablespoons fried garlic

Heat the oil in a wok over a medium-high heat, add the prawns, peppercorns and
2 tablespoons of water. Stir-fry for 5 minutes until the prawns are pink and tender.

Add the chopped garlic, chili jam or paste and kaffir lime leaves and cook for 3 minutes
or until the paste is fragrant.

Stir in the beans, fish sauce and sugar and bring to a boil. Reduce the heat and simmer
for 5 minutes or until the beans are tender. Add the basil leaves and garnish with the
sliced red chili and fried garlic.

Preparation time: 25 minutes – Cooking time: 15 minutes – Serves 4

SWEET CHILI PRAWNS WITH BASIL

Cook the prawns until coated in the sticky-sweet chili sauce.

flat noodles with seafood

1 lb (500 g) fresh flat rice noodles, at room temperature
3–4 tablespoons (45–60 mL) dark soy sauce (enough to coat the noodles)
¼ teaspoon (1 mL) cracked black pepper
3 tablespoons (45 mL) vegetable oil
2 cloves garlic, chopped
10 oz (300 g) prawns, peeled and deveined, tails left intact
6½ oz (200 g) clean baby squid tubes, thinly sliced
6½ oz (200 g) pak choi (bok choy), roughly chopped
1 red bell pepper, sliced
3 oz (100 g) baby corn
¼ cup (60 mL) chicken stock
3 tablespoons (45 mL) oyster sauce
3 tablespoons (45 mL) light soy sauce
1½ tablespoons (22 mL) superfine sugar

Separate the noodles and place them into a bowl, add the soy sauce and pepper and mix to combine. If the noodles have been chilled you will need to rinse them under warm water to soften them but make sure the water isn't too hot or the noodles will break up.

Heat the oil in a wok, add the garlic, prawns and squid and stir-fry for 3 minutes. Add the pak choi (bok choy), red bell pepper and corn and stir-fry for 3 minutes or until the vegetables are soft. Add the stock, oyster sauce, soy sauce and sugar and stir-fry until the noodles are coated in the sauce.

Tip: If at anytime during cooking the noodles stick to the wok add an extra tablespoon of oil.

Preparation time: 25 minutes – Cooking time: 10 minutes – Serves 4

dressed prawn salad

¼ cup (60 mL) fish sauce
¼ cup (60 mL) lime juice
3 tablespoons (45 mL) chili jam (nam prik pao – see page 25)
1½ lb (750 g) raw prawns, peeled and deveined, tails left intact
1 large red chili, seeded and thinly sliced
3 tablespoons (45 mL) finely chopped lemongrass
¼ cup (60 mL) finely chopped red shallots or red onions
½ cup (125 mL) fresh cilantro leaves, chopped
3 tablespoons (45 mL) finely shredded fresh mint leaves
2 spring onions, thinly sliced

Whisk together the fish sauce, lime juice and chili jam in a bowl. Add the prawns and mix well to coat them in the sauce.

Add the chili, lemongrass, shallots or onions, cilantro, mint and spring onions to the bowl and mix well.

Drain the prawns and reserve the sauce. Add the prawns to a wok and cook over a medium heat until pink, which should take 3–5 minutes. Add the reserved sauce and bring to a boil. Transfer to a bowl and refrigerate until cold.

Preparation time: 25 minutes – Cooking time: 5 minutes, plus 4 hours chilling – Serves 4

chicken and duck

Bangkok grilled chicken

4 chicken legs and thighs
¼ cup (60 mL) chopped garlic
¼ cup (60 mL) finely chopped lemongrass
1 teaspoon (5 mL) finely chopped fresh coriander root
2 spring onions, finely chopped
3 tablespoons (45 mL) fish sauce
1½ tablespoons (22 mL) light soy sauce
1½ tablespoons (22 mL) superfine sugar
3 tablespoons (45 mL) lime juice
½ teaspoon (2 mL) ground white pepper

Score the chicken so it will cook evenly. Put the garlic, lemongrass, coriander root and spring onions into a mortar and pestle and pound to form a paste. Transfer to a bowl, stir in the fish sauce, soy sauce, sugar, lime juice and white pepper and mix well to combine. Pour over the chicken and rub the marinade in well. Set aside to marinate for 4 hours or overnight.

Cook the chicken on a lightly oiled barbecue grill, grill pan or under a preheated broiler, turning several times during cooking until tender.

Preparation time: 20 minutes, plus 4–8 hours marinating – Cooking time: 30 minutes – Serves 4

stir-fried chicken and cashews

3 tablespoons (45 mL) vegetable oil
2 Asian shallots, finely sliced
1½ tablespoons (22 mL) fresh galangal, finely sliced
1 lb (500 g) chicken thighs
2 dried chilies, left whole
1 red bell pepper, thinly sliced
3 spring onions, cut into 2 inch/5 cm lengths
3 tablespoons (45 mL) soy sauce
1½ tablespoons (22 mL) grated palm sugar or brown sugar
1½ tablespoons (22 mL) fish sauce
⅔ cup (160 mL) unsalted roasted cashew nuts

TO GARNISH
3 tablespoons (45 mL) fresh cilantro leaves
ground white pepper

Heat the oil in a wok over a medium heat, add the shallots and galangal and stir-fry until light brown. Add the chicken thighs and stir-fry for 4 minutes or until golden brown. Add the chilies, bell pepper and scallions and stir-fry for 3 minutes.

Add the soy sauce, sugar, fish sauce and cashew nuts to the wok and stir-fry for 1–2 minutes or until chicken is cooked.

Transfer to a serving plate and garnish with the cilantro leaves and pepper.

Preparation time:15 minutes – Cooking time: 10 minutes – Serves 4

STIR-FRIED CHICKEN AND CASHEWS

Roast the cashews in a pan on the stove until golden brown.

chicken and duck

chili chicken and basil

3 tablespoons (45 mL) vegetable oil
1½ tablespoons (22 mL) garlic, chopped
1 lb (500 g) boneless chicken thighs, thinly sliced
5 oz (150 g) broccolini, roughly chopped
1 long red chili, seeded and julienned
1 long green chili, seeded and julienned
3 tablespoons (45 mL) chili jam (nam prik pao – see page 25)
3 tablespoons (45 mL) fish sauce
1 cup (250 mL) fresh Thai basil leaves

Heat the oil in a wok over a high heat, add the garlic and stir-fry for 1 minute. Add the chicken and stir-fry, tossing constantly, for 1–2 minutes or until the chicken is golden. Toss in the broccolini, red and green chili, chili jam and fish sauce and stir-fry until the chicken is tender, which takes about 5 minutes. Toss through the basil leaves until they are wilted and serve the dish immediately.

Preparation time: 10 minutes – Cooking time: 10 minutes – Serves 2–4

fragrant green chicken curry

1½ tablespoons (22 mL) vegetable oil
14 oz (400 g) chicken breast fillets, sliced
1½–3 tablespoons (22–45 mL) green curry paste (see page 22)
2 cups (500 mL) coconut milk
2 kaffir lime leaves, stems removed and torn into pieces
4 Thai eggplants or 1 large eggplant, cut into quarters
1¼ oz (50 g) pea eggplant (optional)
3½ oz (100 g) snake beans or green beans, sliced
3½ oz (100 g) can bamboo shoots, drained
¼ cup (60 mL) fresh Thai basil leaves
3 tablespoons (45 mL) fish sauce
3 tablespoons (45 mL) grated palm sugar or brown sugar
1 teaspoon (5 mL) lime juice
fresh cilantro leaves, to serve

Heat the oil in a wok, add the chicken and stir-fry over a medium-high heat for
5 minutes or until browned. Add the curry paste and stir-fry until fragrant. Stir in
the coconut milk and lime leaves and bring to a boil before cooking for 5 minutes.

Reduce the heat to a simmer and add the eggplants, beans and bamboo shoots and
simmer for 15 minutes or until the beans are tender. Stir in the basil leaves, fish sauce
and sugar and cook for a further 5 minutes. Turn off the heat and stir in the lime juice.

Serve topped with the cilantro leaves.

Preparation time: 20 minutes – Cooking time: 30 minutes – Serves 4

chicken and duck

chicken pad thai

8 oz (250 g) thin rice stick noodles
3 tablespoons (45 mL) vegetable oil
10 oz (300 g) chicken breast fillets, sliced
3½ oz (100 g) firm tofu, drained and thinly sliced
3 cloves garlic, chopped
3 tablespoons (45 mL) dried shrimp (optional)
2 cups (500 mL) bean sprouts
½ cup (125 mL) fish sauce
3 tablespoons (45 mL) superfine sugar
5½ tablespoons (82 mL) tamarind water
2 eggs, lightly beaten
¼ cup (60 mL) chopped roasted peanuts
3 tablespoons (45 mL) garlic chives, cut into 1¼ inch (3 cm) pieces

TO GARNISH
1 lime, cut into wedges
1 cucumber, peeled and sliced

Put the rice stick noodles into a bowl, cover with cold water and allow to stand for
20 minutes or until soft. Drain well.

Heat the oil in a wok, add the chicken and tofu and stir-fry over a high heat for
5 minutes or until the chicken is browned. Add the garlic and shrimp and cook for
2 minutes. Add the noodles and stir-fry until soft. Add the bean sprouts and stir-fry
until the beans sprouts are soft.

Whisk together the fish sauce, sugar and tamarind and add the mixture to the wok.
Stir-fry for 5 minutes or until the noodles absorb the sauce.

Push the noodles up one side of the wok, add the eggs and cook, stirring, until the eggs
are scrambled. Add the peanuts and chives and combine with the noodles and eggs.
Stir-fry for 2 minutes.

Serve plates of the pad thai, each accompanied with a wedge of lime and slices of peeled
cucumber.

Preparation time: 30 minutes, plus 20 minutes soaking – Cooking time: 15 minutes – Serves 4

chicken and duck

yellow chicken curry

3 tablespoons (45 mL) vegetable oil
3–4 tablespoons (45–60 mL) yellow curry paste (see page 25)
1 teaspoon (5 mL) yellow curry powder
1 cup (250 mL) coconut milk
8 chicken drumsticks
2 potatoes, parboiled and cut into large pieces
1 onion, sliced
4½ oz (130 g) can bamboo shoots, drained
1 cup (250 mL) chicken stock
1½ tablespoons (22 mL) fish sauce
3 tablespoons (45 mL) tamarind water
3 tablespoons (45 mL) grated palm sugar or brown sugar

Heat the oil in a wok, add the curry paste and curry powder and cook for 2 minutes or until the paste is fragrant. Pour in the coconut milk, including the thick cream from the top of the can, and bring to a boil, stirring constantly, until the oil starts to separate from the cream.

Score the chicken drumsticks. Add the chicken, potatoes, onion, bamboo shoots and stock to the wok and simmer, covered, for 30–40 minutes or until the chicken is tender.

Add the fish sauce, tamarind and sugar and cook for a further 5 minutes or until the chicken is tender.

Preparation time: 30 minutes – Cooking time: 45 minutes – Serves 4

duck and pineapple curry

3 tablespoons (45 mL) vegetable oil
3–4 tablespoons (45–60 mL) red curry paste (see page 24)
2 cups (500 mL) coconut milk
1 cup (250 mL) chicken stock
2 stalks lemongrass, bruised
½ Chinese roast duck, cut into bite-sized pieces
4 spring onions, sliced
3 kaffir lime leaves, stems discarded and leaves torn
6 cherry tomatoes
4 oz (400 g) fresh pineapple, cut into bite-sized pieces
3 tablespoons (45 mL) fish sauce
3 tablespoons (45 mL) grated palm sugar or brown sugar
3 tablespoons (45 mL) fresh basil leaves

Heat the oil in a wok, add the paste and cook until fragrant. Pour in the coconut milk, including the thick cream from the top of the can, and cook, stirring constantly, for 5 minutes or until the oil starts to separate from the cream.

Add the stock, lemongrass, duck, spring onions, lime leaves, tomatoes and pineapple to the wok and bring to the boil, reduce the heat and simmer, uncovered, for 15 minutes.

Add the fish sauce, sugar and basil leaves and cook for 5 minutes.

Preparation time: 20 minutes – Cooking time: 25 minutes – Serves 4

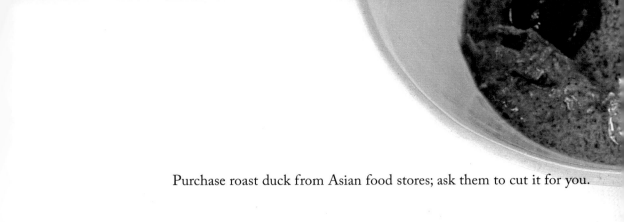

Purchase roast duck from Asian food stores; ask them to cut it for you.

chicken and duck

ginger chicken and snow pea stir-fry

3 tablespoons (45 mL) vegetable oil
1 lb (500 g) chicken breast, sliced
3 tablespoons (45 mL) finely shredded ginger
2 cloves garlic, chopped
2 stalks celery, thinly sliced
4½ oz (130 g) can water chestnuts, halved
7 oz (200 g) snow peas
2 spring onions, cut into 1¼ inch (3 cm) pieces
¼ cup (60 mL) soy sauce
1½ tablespoons (22 mL) superfine sugar
½ cup (125 mL) chicken stock
1½ tablespoons (22 mL) Chinese cooking wine

Heat the oil in a wok, add the chicken breast and stir-fry over a medium-high heat for 5 minutes or until the chicken browns.

Add the ginger, garlic, celery and water chestnuts to the wok and cook for 3 minutes. Add the snow peas, spring onions, soy sauce, sugar, stock and cooking wine and cook, stirring constantly, until the sauce boils.

Preparation time: 15 minutes – Cooking time: 15 minutes – Serves 4

chicken spicy noodles

1½ tablespoons (22 mL) vegetable oil
4 cloves garlic, crushed
1 teaspoon (5 mL) dried chili
2 Asian shallots, finely chopped
1 lb (500 g) chicken breast, sliced
1 red bell pepper, sliced
3½ oz (100 g) asparagus, sliced
3½ oz (100 g) broccolini, roughly chopped
3 tablespoons (45 mL) fish sauce
1½ tablespoons (22 mL) grated palm sugar or brown sugar
1½ tablespoons (22 mL) tamarind water
14 oz (400 g) hokkien noodles
½ cup (125 mL) fresh cilantro leaves
lime wedges, to serve

Heat the oil in a wok over a medium heat, add the garlic, chili and shallots and stir-fry for 2 minutes. Add the chicken and stir-fry for 5 minutes or until the chicken is cooked. Add the red pepper, asparagus and broccolini and stir-fry for 3 minutes. Add the fish sauce, sugar, tamarind water and noodles and stir-fry for 2 minutes. Toss through the cilantro leaves and serve immediately, with the lime wedges.

Preparation time: 15 minutes — Cooking time: 15 minutes — Serves 4

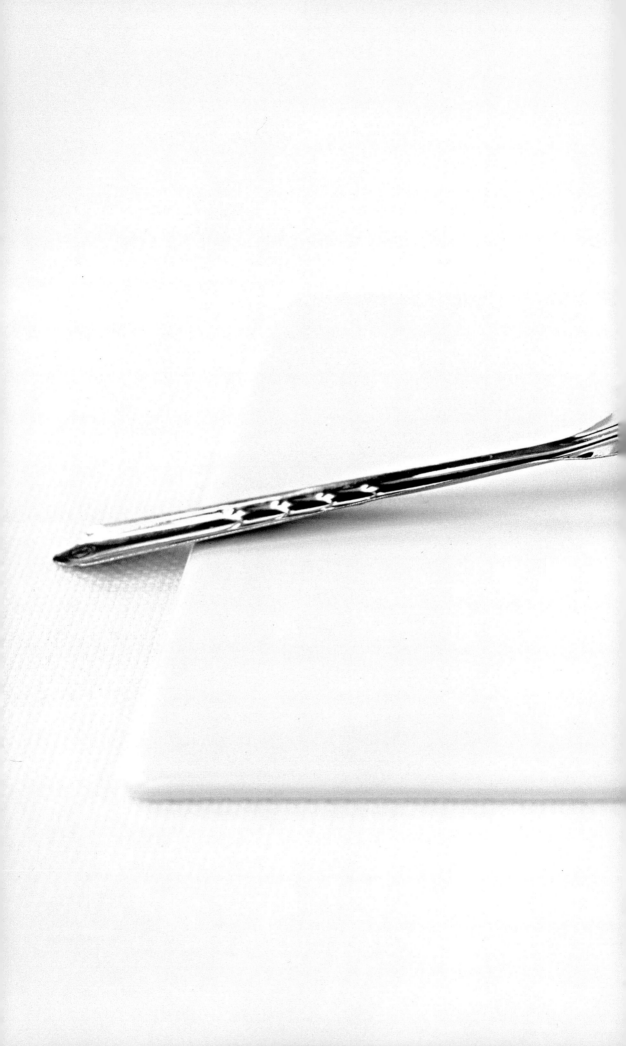

meat

Penang beef curry

3 tablespoons (45 mL) vegetable oil
1½–3 tablespoons (22–45 mL) penang curry paste (see page 24)
3 kaffir lime leaves, stem removed and finely sliced
10 oz (300 g) rump steak, sliced
1 cup (250 mL) coconut milk
3 tablespoons (45 mL) fish sauce
1½ tablespoons (22 mL) grated palm sugar or brown sugar
3 tablespoons (45 mL) fresh Thai basil leaves
½ teaspoon (2 mL) freshly ground black pepper
1 large red chili, seeded and finely sliced, to garnish

Heat the oil in a wok, add the curry paste and lime leaves and cook over a medium heat until the curry paste is fragrant.

Add the beef and half the coconut milk and stir-fry until the beef is cooked. Add the remaining coconut milk and cook, stirring constantly, until the coconut milk boils. Stir in the fish sauce, sugar, basil and black pepper and simmer for a further 3 minutes. Garnish with the red chili.

Preparation time: 15 minutes – Cooking time: 15 minutes – Serves 4

stir-fried noodles with beef and oyster sauce

1½ tablespoons (22 mL) peanut oil
10 oz (300 g) rump steak, thinly sliced
2 cloves garlic, chopped
1 red bell pepper, sliced
3½ oz (100 g) shiitake mushrooms, sliced
10 oz (300 g) hokkien noodles
7 oz (200 g) Chinese broccoli or pak choi (bok choy), roughly chopped
3 tablespoons (45 mL) soy sauce
¼ cup (60 mL) oyster sauce
2 teaspoons (10 mL) superfine sugar
½ teaspoon (2 mL) white pepper

Heat the oil in a wok, add the steak and stir-fry over a high heat until browned. Add the garlic, red bell pepper and shiitake mushrooms and stir-fry for 3 minutes or until the shiitake are tender. Add the noodles and broccoli or pak choi (bok choy) and stir-fry for 3 minutes or until the noodles soften.

Combine the sauces, sugar and pepper and add these to the wok. Stir-fry until the sauce boils then remove from the heat.

Preparation time: 20 minutes – Cooking time: 10 minutes – Serves 4

Chiang Mai pork curry

1 lb (500 g) pork fillet, cubed
3 tablespoons (45 mL) fish sauce
3 tablespoons (45 mL) grated palm sugar or brown sugar
3 tablespoons (45 mL) red curry paste (see page 24)
1 teaspoon (5 mL) Indian curry powder or curry powder
3 tablespoons (45 mL) vegetable oil
½ cup (125 mL) roasted peanuts
1 oz (30 g) fresh ginger, peeled and julienned
3 tablespoons (45 mL) tamarind water

Put the pork, fish sauce, sugar, curry paste and curry powder into a bowl, cover and allow to stand for 30 minutes.

Heat the oil in a wok, add the marinated pork and any marinade and stir-fry for 5 minutes or until the pork changes color. Add 2 cups (500 mL) water, the peanuts, ginger and tamarind water and bring to a boil. Reduce the heat and simmer for 20 minutes or until the sauce has thickened.

Preparation time: 15 minutes, plus 30 minutes standing – Cooking time: 20 minutes – Serves 4–6

STIR-FRIED NOODLES WITH BEEF AND OYSTER SAUCE

This curry is lighter than most of its coconut cream counterparts.

CHAING MAI PORK CURRY

meat

larb moo

1 lb (500 g) ground pork
¼ teaspoon (1 mL) chili powder
3 tablespoons (45 mL) chopped red shallots or red onions
¼ cup (60 mL) fish sauce
¼ cup (60 mL) lime juice
3 tablespoons (45 mL) chopped fresh mint
3 tablespoons (45 mL) chopped fresh cilantro

TO SERVE
1 Lebanese cucumber, sliced
1 cup (250 mL) shredded Chinese cabbage

Put the ground pork, chili and shallots or onions into a wok, add 2 tablespoons of water and stir-fry over a medium heat until the pork is cooked but not browned.

Turn off the heat and stir in the fish sauce, lime juice, mint and cilantro. Serve warm with sliced cucumber and shredded Chinese cabbage.

Preparation time: 10 minutes – Cooking time: 15 minutes – Serves 4

northern-style barbecue ribs

1½ tablespoons (22 mL) finely shredded fresh ginger
1 teaspoon (5 mL) white pepper
¼ teaspoon (1 mL) five spice powder
1 teaspoon (5 mL) sea salt
½ cup (125 mL) soy sauce
¼ cup (60 mL) fish sauce
¼ cup (60 mL) grated palm sugar or brown sugar
¼ cup (60 mL) whisky
2 lb (1 kg) pork spare ribs (American style with bone in)

Put the ginger, white pepper, five spice powder, salt, soy sauce, fish sauce, sugar and whisky into a large bowl and mix until the sugar dissolves. Add the pork ribs and massage the marinade into the ribs to coat them. Cover and refrigerate for 4 hours or overnight.

Preheat a grill to high. Remove the ribs from the marinade and place onto a baking tray, grill, turning and basting several times, until tender.

Preparation time: 15 minutes, plus 4–8 hours marinating – Cooking time: 20 minutes – Serves 6

130

meat

masaman beef curry

3 tablespoons (45 mL) vegetable oil
3–5½ tablespoons (45–82 mL) masaman curry paste (see page 24)
14 oz (400 g) rump steak, cubed
2 potatoes, parboiled and cut into quarters
1 onion, chopped
2 cups (500 mL) coconut milk
1 teaspoon (5 mL) sea salt
3 tablespoons (45 mL) grated palm sugar or brown sugar
1½ tablespoons (22 mL) fish sauce
3 tablespoons (45 mL) tamarind water

Heat the oil in a wok, add the curry paste and cook over a low heat for 3 minutes or until fragrant. Increase the heat to medium, add the beef, potatoes and onion and cook until the beef browns.

Stir in the coconut milk, salt, sugar, fish sauce and bring to a boil. Reduce the heat and simmer for 15 minutes or until the potatoes are cooked. Add the tamarind water and cook for a further 5 minutes.

Preparation time: 20 minutes – Cooking time: 25 minutes – Serves 4

meat

stir-fried pork with soy

3 tablespoons (45 mL) vegetable oil
1 lb (500 g) pork fillet, sliced
1 onion, thinly sliced
2 cloves garlic, chopped
2 large red chilies, seeded and thinly sliced
¼ cup (60 mL) light soy sauce
1 teaspoon (5 mL) superfine sugar
½ cup (125 mL) fresh Thai basil leaves

Heat the oil in a wok, add the pork and stir-fry over a high heat until brown and tender. Add the onion and garlic and cook for 3 minutes or until the onion is soft and golden.

Add the chilies, soy sauce and sugar and cook until the sauce is heated through. Add the basil leaves and cook for a further 1 minute.

Preparation time: 10 minutes – Cooking time: 10 minutes – Serves 4

meat

grilled Thai beef salad

1 lb (500 g) piece rib-eye fillet
1½ tablespoons (22 mL) oyster sauce
1 Lebanese cucumber or cucumber, seeded and sliced
1/2 cup (125 mL) fresh cilantro leaves
1/2 cup (125 mL) fresh mint leaves
1 large red chili, seeded and finely sliced
2 Asian shallots, finely sliced
3 tablespoons (45 mL) grated palm sugar or brown sugar
¼ cup (60 mL) lime juice
¼ cup (60 mL) fish sauce

TO GARNISH
¼ cup (60 mL) unsalted roasted peanuts, roughly chopped
3 tablespoons (45 mL) fried shallots

Rub the beef with the oyster sauce. Cook on a barbecue grill or griddle pan for
3 minutes each side or until medium rare. Remove from the pan and leave to rest for
10 minutes before slicing thinly. Transfer the beef to a bowl and add the cucumber,
cilantro, mint, chili and shallots.

In a small bowl mix together the sugar, lime juice and fish sauce until the sugar
dissolves. Drizzle the dressing over the beef dish and gently toss the ingredients
together. To serve divide the salad among 4 plates and sprinkle with peanuts and
fried shallots.

Preparation time: 15 minutes – Cooking time: 10 minutes, plus 10 minutes resting – Serves 4

desserts

banana fritters

FOR THE SAUCE
½ cup (125 mL) grated palm sugar or brown sugar
⅓ cup + 1 tablespoon (100 mL) light cream
⅓ cup + 1 tablespoon (100 mL) coconut milk

FOR THE BATTER
¾ cup (185 mL) all-purpose flour
⅔ cup (160 mL) rice flour
1 teaspoon (5 mL) baking powder
3 tablespoons (45 mL) superfine sugar
½ teaspoon (2 mL) sea salt
1 tablespoon (15 mL) roasted sesame seeds
1¾ oz (50 g) desiccated coconut
1 cup (250 mL) soda water

8 bananas, peeled and cut in half
2 cups (500 mL) vegetable oil

Place the sugar, cream and coconut milk into a small saucepan and heat over a medium heat. Bring to a boil and simmer until the sauce becomes thick. Set aside.

In a mixing bowl add the all-purpose flour, rice flour, baking powder, sugar, salt, sesame seeds and coconut and mix together well. Gradually whisk in the soda water to make a thick smooth batter. Coat the bananas in the batter.

Heat the oil in a wok or saucepan over a medium heat and deep-fry the bananas for 3–5 minutes or until crisp and golden. Remove and drain on absorbent kitchen paper. Serve the bananas with the sauce to the side.

Preparation time: 20 minutes – Cooking time: 30 minutes – Makes 16 fritters

desserts

This fantastic moist cake will keep for several days in an airtight container.

banana coconut cake

1⅓ cups (330 mL) shredded coconut
½ cup (125 mL) coconut milk
5 large ripe bananas, mashed
1 cup (250 mL) rice flour
¼ cup (60 mL) arrowroot
½ cup (125 mL) superfine sugar
3 tablespoons (45 mL) sweetened condensed milk

TO SERVE
ice cream

Preheat the oven to 350°F (180°C). Grease and line an 8 inch (20 cm) cake tin. Put the coconut and coconut milk into a bowl and allow to stand for 10 minutes.

Add the bananas, flour, arrowroot, sugar and condensed milk to the bowl and mix to combine. Spoon the mixture into the prepared cake tin and bake for 50 minutes. Allow to cool before turning out. Serve warm with ice cream.

Preparation time: 15 minutes, plus 10 minutes standing – Cooking time: 50 minutes, plus 10 minutes cooling – Serves 4

banana pancakes

1 cup (250 mL) all-purpose white flour
pinch of sea salt
1 cup (250 mL) milk
2 tablespoons (30 mL) melted butter
2 eggs, lightly beaten
butter to cook with
4 bananas, thinly sliced

TO SERVE
condensed milk (optional)

Mix the flour and salt together in a large bowl. In another bowl mix the milk, melted butter and eggs together. Add these slowly to the dry mixture and mix until well combined. Heat a little butter in a frying pan over a medium heat, pour a quarter of the batter into the pan and cook until bubbles appear on the surface.

Place a quarter of the banana onto half of the cooked mixture and then turn it over. Cook for another 2 minutes or until the mixture is cooked. Remove from the pan and top with the bananas.

If not serving immediately keep warm in a moderate oven and cook the remaining mixture. Serve the pancakes accompanied by the condensed milk (if using).

Preparation time: 10 minutes – Cooking time: 25 minutes – Serves 4

banana in sweet coconut milk

6 small lady finger bananas or small bananas
2¾ cups (685 mL) coconut milk
1 pandanus leaf (optional)
½ cup (125 mL) granulated sugar
½ teaspoon (2 mL) sea salt

Peel the bananas and cut in half lengthwise and then in half again.

Put the coconut milk and pandanus (if using) into a pan and cook, stirring, until the coconut milk is about to boil. Reduce the heat to a simmer and add the bananas, sugar and salt. Simmer gently for 3–5 minutes. Do not overcook as the bananas are meant to be firm.

Preparation time: 5 minutes – Cooking time: 10 minutes – Serves 4

The black sticky rice will thicken on standing, and is delicious hot or cold.

BLACK STICKY RICE

black sticky rice

1½ cups (375 mL) black glutinous rice
2 cups (500 mL) coconut milk
½ cup (125 mL) grated palm sugar or brown sugar

Put the rice into a bowl, cover with cold water and allow to soak overnight.

Put the rice and 6 cups (1.5 L) cold water into a pan and bring to the boil before simmering for 20 minutes. Drain.

Put the coconut milk and sugar into a pan, stir until the sugar dissolves, add the rice and cook for 10 minutes over a medium heat until heated through.

Preparation time: 10 minutes, plus overnight soaking – Cooking time: 30 minutes – Serves 4–6

coconut custard

1¾ cups (400 mL) coconut milk
3 eggs, lightly beaten
¼ cup (60 mL) grated palm sugar or brown sugar

TO SERVE
3 tablespoons (45 mL) shredded coconut, toasted

Put the coconut milk, eggs and sugar into a bowl and whisk to combine.

Pour the mixture into four ½ cup (125 mL) ramekins and place into a bamboo steamer over a wok of simmering water.

Cover and steam for 30 minutes or until set. Serve topped with toasted coconut.

Preparation time: 10 minutes – Cooking time: 30 minutes – Serves 4

COCONUT CUSTARD

desserts

sticky rice with mango

2 cups (500 mL) white sticky rice
1 cup (250 mL) coconut milk
¼ cup (60 mL) superfine sugar
pinch of sea salt

TO SERVE
2 mangoes, sliced

Soak the rice in cold water overnight. Rinse and drain well. Put the rice into a bamboo steamer lined with parchment paper that has been pierced with several holes.

Place the steamer into a wok over simmering water, cover and cook for 20 minutes or until the rice is cooked. Transfer to a bowl.

Add the coconut milk, sugar and salt to the bowl and mix until the sugar dissolves. Set aside until the rice has absorbed the coconut milk, which takes around 15 minutes. Serve the sticky rice with the mango.

Preparation time: 5 minutes, plus overnight soaking – Cooking time: 20 minutes, plus 15 minutes standing – Serves 4

BASIL Thais use a variety of basil but most commonly sweet Thai basil. Thai, or sweet, basil has green variegated leaves with slightly purple stems and a strong aniseed flavor. It is widely used in curries, stir-fries and soups and is usually added towards the end of cooking or scattered over the top of dishes as a garnish. If you cannot find Thai basil then substitute normal basil leaves.

BAMBOO SHOOTS Most often sold in cans, these can be thin slices or simply a cone shaped root that has been cut in half. Rinsed and drained before using, bamboo shoots are delicious in curries and stir-fries.

CHILI

SMALL RED Also known as bird's eye chilies, use these with caution and remember that the heat is in the seed and membrane. For a hot spicy dish chop, for a milder dish halve the chili and for a very mild dish leave them whole.

LARGE RED Widely used in Thai cooking, large red chilies are not used for their heat, but for their visual appeal. Remove the seeds and finely shred to garnish salad, soups and curries. For more spice leave the seeds in.

SMALL GREEN Small green chilies are milder than small red chilies. They can be used to make green chili paste and are not usually as hot as large green chilies.

LARGE GREEN Large green chilies are hotter than large red chilies. They can be used to make green curry paste.

DRIED LARGE RED These are not so spicy as a lot of them have the seeds removed before drying. Soak them in hot water for 10 minutes before using, then drain and chop. Dried chilies are used to make red curry pastes.

CHINESE CABBAGE Also known as wombok, Chinese cabbage has a delicate mustard flavor and is widely used in Thai cooking in salads, soups and stir-fries. Other curly leaf cabbage may be used instead, but be sure to finely shred it.

CHILI JAM Also known as nam prik prao, this is used in stir-fries and soups and is quite sweet rather than being fiery. If you don't want to make your own it is sold in bottles as chili bean paste in soya bean (soybean) oil.

CILANTRO Also known as Chinese parsley, this is widely used in Thai cooking. The root is often used in making curry pastes and garlic and pepper paste. It has a delicious peppery flavor. Store it wrapped in damp absorbent kitchen paper in an airtight container or plastic bag. The leaves are used for flavoring and in curry pastes – mainly to add color to green curry paste.

COCONUT MILK/ COCONUT CREAM These days when you buy a can of coconut milk or coconut cream it is difficult to tell the difference. If you want to use coconut cream, do not shake the can and remove the thick cream from the top of the can with a spoon.

CORIANDER SEED Coriander seeds feature strongly in Thai cooking. They are often used in curry pastes. The seeds need to be roasted over a low heat in a wok before crushing. Roast only the quantities you need at the time as they are best used fresh.

CURRY POWDER Indian curry powder is used in the food of South Thailand. It is an essential ingredient in yellow curry paste and often appears in chicken and fish dishes.

DRIED SHRIMP Tiny dried shrimp are widely used in Thai cooking in salads, soups, stir-fries and noodle dishes. Store the shrimp in the refrigerator to prevent them from spoiling. Quality varies quite widely – select the naturally colored dried pink shrimp, as some brands have been artificially colored.

EGGPLANT

PEA These look like small peas and come in small clusters. They can be added whole to curries, soups and stir-fries and are crunchy on the outside and slightly bitter.

THAI These eggplants are round golf-ball size eggplants that can be either green and white or pale purple and white. They discolor quickly after they have been cut so soak them in lemon juice and water before you add them to your dishes. They are most often used in curries – particularly green.

FISH SAUCE Also known as nam pla, fish sauce is a smelly thin brown liquid that is widely used in Thai cooking to salt and season dishes. It is made from fermented or pickled fish or prawns. It is sold in bottles – I recommend the Squid brand as it is not too salty. Vegetarians can use light soy sauce instead.

GARLIC

THAI GARLIC is smaller than the ones we get in the West and slightly more pungent. Try to purchase small young cloves with soft skins if you can't get Thai garlic.

DEEP-FRIED GARLIC This is available in jars from Asian stores and it is used to flavor soups and stocks, stir-fries, salad and noodle dishes. If you have time there is nothing better than homemade fried garlic. Slice the unpeeled garlic into paper-thin slices and deep-fry until crisp and golden brown. Drain on absorbent kitchen paper.

GALANGAL Widely used in Thai cooking, galangal is a member of the ginger family, but its flavor is much more pungent. Young galangal is cream with pinkish stems and is great for flavoring soups and is probably best known as the ingredient in Tom Kai Gai. Older galangal develops a pinkish tinge and starts to dry out – this is when it is ideal to use in curry pastes.

GINGER This is not widely used in Thai cooking and most of the dishes it appears in are those of Chinese origin. Use it on steamed fish, soups and salads. It is often used to remove the fishy flavor from dishes.

KAFFIR LIME The grated zest of the kaffir lime is used in some green curry pastes. If you can't find the limes just omit them from the recipe.

KAFFIR LIME LEAVES These leaves (2 leaves joined together is counted in a recipe as 1 leaf) are widely used in Thai cooking. Remove the tough middle stem and tear the leaves for soups and curries, finely shred them in salads and stir-fries. Fresh leaves can be frozen. Dried leaves can be used instead but they don't have the wonderful pungent lime flavor of the fresh.

LEMONGRASS Also known as citronella, this long, fragrant, grass-like plant is used in soups, curry pastes and tea. Remove any dry outer leaves and use only the bottom white base. Discard the top green blades or use them to make tea. Lemongrass can be sliced, chopped finely or pounded in a mortar and pestle before cooking. Dried lemongrass has a much more subtle flavor and needs to be soaked in warm water before using.

NOODLES
FRESH RICE These are available from Asian stores. If you can buy them at room temperature use them on the same day. Some shops store them in the refrigerator section, but this makes them brittle and difficult to separate and you will need to bring them to room

temperature before use. They are sold in large sheets that can be sliced into thick noodles or buy them as ready-cut noodles.

FRESH HOKKIEN These fresh egg noodles are more Chinese than Thai but are often used in stir-fries. They are precooked so do not need to be soaked, just separated before being added to the wok.

DRIED RICE STICK The pad thai noodles, dried rice noodles come in a variety of widths. Soak them in cold water if you have time as this will stop them overcooking and falling apart when you stir-fry them.

DRIED RICE VERMICELLI These fine rice noodles are often confused with glass noodles but they are whiter when rehydrated. They can be deep-fried from their dried state or soaked in cold water before using in soups and salads.

DRIED GLASS Glass noodles are transparent noodles made from mung beans that are used in soups, salads and spring rolls. Soak them in hot water before using.

OYSTER MUSHROOMS These flat mushrooms are used in soups, salads and stir-fries. They require very little cooking and can be added towards the end of cooking.

OYSTER SAUCE Although Chinese in origin, oyster sauce is now widely used in Thai stir-fries. Vegetarians can use mushroom oyster sauce as a substitute. Store the opened bottle in the refrigerator to prevent a mold forming on the surface.

PALM SUGAR This is made from the sap of the trunk of the coconut palm or sugar palm. Thais use palm sugar to sweeten most of their curries and desserts. It is sold in blocks or jars and needs to be shaved from the block using a knife or, depending on how firm it is, you can often grate it. Brown

sugar may be used as a substitute.

PANDANUS LEAF This long glossy leaf, from the pandanus palm, is used to flavor desserts in Thailand. It is usually tied in a knot and used to perfume dishes. Asian stores will sell it fresh or frozen. If you purchase the frozen leaves, remove what you need then refreeze the rest.

PAPAYA Green unripe papaya is used to make Som Tam – green papaya salad. Select firm papaya and store in the refrigerator to stop it ripening.

PEPPERCORNS
FRESH GREEN Long strands of fresh green peppercorns are available in the refrigerator section of Asian food stores. These are the fresh young pepper, before it is dried and becomes black pepper. Green peppercorns add a mild peppery flavor to a dish, but if you can't find them you can add some black peppercorns. Bottled green peppercorns have been pickled in a brine so they are not a suitable substitute.

WHITE Widely used in Thai cooking, white peppercorns should only be ground just before use to keep them as fresh as possible. Try to find Thai white peppercorns, which are slightly different to Western ones – they are smaller with black streaks.

RICE
JASMINE RICE This is a fragrant long-grain rice that is highly prized in Thai cooking. It is steamed and served at all meals. Rinse the rice before using. Basmati rice has a totally different flavor and is not really considered to be a substitute.

BLACK GLUTINOUS Black sticky rice is only used to make desserts. Like white sticky rice, it needs to be soaked in cold water overnight before cooking.

STICKY RICE Mainly eaten in the north of Thailand now, sticky rice is still always served as an accompaniment to Som

Tam – green papaya salad. It can be served as a sweet or savory rice. It needs to be soaked in cold water overnight before cooking to soften the grain.

RICE PAPER WRAPPERS Dried rice paper wrappers come in rounds and squares and in a range of sizes. They are fragile and need to be soaked one at a time in warm water for seconds until soft.

SHALLOTS Asian shallots are smaller than French shallots and come in small purplish bunches that resemble garlic cloves. Red onions may be used as a substitute. Shallots are used in curry pastes, soups and salads. You can deep-fry them and add them to salads or use them as a garnish. Deep-fried shallots can also be purchased in jars in Asian stores.

SHRIMP PASTE Also known as gapi, this pungent paste has been salted and fermented then left in the sun for up to a year to mature. It is sold in small tubs or in a block – I prefer the tubs as they are easier to seal and keep the odor enclosed. It can be added to dishes as it is or wrap it in foil and roast it to develop the flavor. Store it in an airtight container in the refrigerator – it lasts forever.

SNAKE BEANS These long, whip-like beans are used in fish cakes, salads, soups and curries. They tend to toughen and dry out as they get older so try to purchase young ones if you can. Green beans may be substituted.

SOY SAUCE Thais use light soy sauce rather than dark soy in their cooking. It is used in marinades, salad dressings and in stir-fries.

SPRING ROLL WRAPPERS These wrappers are usually sold frozen and need to be defrosted before you can use them. Gently separate the wrappers and keep any you are not using immediately covered with a damp tea towel to stop them from drying out while you start to roll your spring rolls.

SWEET CHILI SAUCE This is a very mild sweet condiment that is widely used in Thai cuisine. It can be used for dipping fish cakes, spring rolls or other appetizers and is often served with fried chicken. It is sold in tall bottles and is available in Asian food stores. Shake the bottle well before using as the chilli tends to gather at the top of the bottle.

TAMARIND This is a major seasoning ingredient in Thai cooking. It is used to give the distinctive sour taste to dishes, most notably Tom Yum Goong (Sour Prawn Soup). It is purchased as a compressed block of pulp wrapped in plastic and you simply make the water as you need it. To do this, break off a piece of pulp and cover it with an equal amount of warm water, allow it to stand for 10 minutes then gently squeeze the pulp to dislodge the seeds. Pass it through a sieve and discard the fibre and seeds.

TOFU Also known as beancurd, tofu comes in a variety of textures – from soft to firm – and is available in the refrigerator section of shops. Remove it from its water and if you find it is still too soft weigh it down to remove some of the excess moisture (I do this by placing it in between two chopping boards). Softer tofu is used in soups and desserts and the firmer types are added to stir-fries and noodles dishes.

TURMERIC Fresh turmeric is most often used in the cuisine of South Thailand. It is a major ingredient in yellow curry paste and looks like mini ginger with a bright orange center. Use gloves when preparing dishes with it as it stains everything it comes into contact with. Powdered turmeric may be used as a substitute, but in much smaller quantities as the flavor is much stronger.

acknowledgements

Khawp khun kha – that's Thai for "thanks" (if you are a woman). To Catie Ziller, patient, inspirational and visionary publisher. To Deirdre Rooney, my ridiculously dedicated, hard-working, talented photographer and designer who experienced more than her fair share of computer and personal challenges while shooting this book.

Thanks to my kitchen angels – Alice Hart for all the wonderful work you did on making the recipes in the book look so lovely and to Harriet Eastwood and Mary Wall for helping out on a day here and there. To Claire Musters, my inquisitive and thorough editor – I hope I didn't drive you nuts with the coconut milk/cream thing. Tracey Gordon, my amazing Kiwi kitchen wizard, thanks for the lovely recipes and super dooper prepping work you do with me day in day out.

Thanks to my sister Paulie for picking me up on the motorbike from the Thai cooking school each day and ensuring we both didn't end up in hospital. Thanks also to the staff at SITCA on Koh Samui, my favorite cooking school, for all the special tips and takeaway packages.

And finally the hugest heartfelt thanks to Matt, Relle, Rarnie and Nath for minding Pridey so I could come and shoot these books – I owe you a new backyard and a lifetime of Thai dinners.

This edition published in North America in 2009 by Whitecap Books Ltd.

For more information, contact Whitecap Books, 351 Lynn Avenue, North Vancouver, British Columbia, Canada V7J 2C4. Visit our website at www.whitecap.ca.

ISBN: 978-1-55285-970-4

Printed in China

09 10 11 12 13 5 4 3 2 1